# Still Howling

Mary Dezember

Copyright © 2016 Mary Dezember
All rights reserved.

No part of this book may be reproduced in any manner without written permission from the author, except for passages in critical articles and reviews and for educational purposes. Individual poems, if the author is credited, may be used for educational purposes.

The author may be contacted at:
dezemberpoetry@gmail.com

Library of Congress Control Number: 2016916617
CreateSpace Independent Publishing Platform, North Charleston, SC

ISBN-13: 978-1536984569
ISBN-10: 1536984566

Cover Art: *Hope* by Steve Dezember II
Used with permission.

For my children,
all five:
because of you
I know life's purest poetry


For my father,
Garnett C Dezember,
who lovingly encouraged me to think,
and to communicate,
critically and independently


For my mother,
Elaine Jewell Schaffer Dezember,
who loved me with a devoted mother's love,
and who, by example, taught me
the power of faith
and the preciousness of life


For my amazing, incredible, inspiring nephew and niece,
Steve and Hope Dezember


For poet extraordinaire,
Allen Ginsberg,
in celebration of the 60th anniversary year of the publication of
"Howl" and "Footnote to Howl," 1956, the year of my birth


And for my beautiful and resilient soul sister,
Galaxy Dancer

# Acknowledgements

The author gratefully acknowledges the following publications
in which the following poems, or versions of them, first appeared:

*Adobe Walls:*
"Pure Poetry and Art,"
which was published in a longer version titled "Excerpt"

*Cacti Fur:*
"Still Howling"
"Endnote to Still Howling"

*Fixed and Free Anthology:*
"Prologue to Rosalind Franklin Speaks:"
"Sun Shining Through"
"A Wedding"

*Nakedness: Poems of Sensuality and Spirituality, CD:*
"The Dead Don't Sin"
"Worship, Discovery and Reclamation"

"Still Howling" and "Endnote to Still Howling" are the First Place Winner of the *Best Beat Poem Contest, 2016,* sponsored by *Beatlick Press*

The author wishes to thank the following loved ones for your
editorial and artistic contributions and caring support:

Elaine Dezember Ritchel
Sean Dezember Ritchel
Galaxy Dancer
Steve Dezember II
Hope Cross Dezember


The author also wishes to thank:

Allen Ginsberg
Walt Whitman
Lawrence Ferlinghetti
Nancy J. Peters
Rosalind Franklin
Georgia O'Keeffe

You take what life gives you,
And you make it work.

— Hope Cross Dezember

# Contents

Pure Poetry and Art  9
Sun Shining Through  11
Prologue to Rosalind Franklin Speaks:  13
Rosalind Franklin Speaks  14
Whose Art?  16
Georgia O'Keeffe's *Black Iris III*, 1926  17
Dream Animals  18
Clearstory  19
A Wedding  21
2 a.m. Snowflakes in March in New Mexico  22
Canvas of Life, Look Closely  25
Walking a Bridge of Fire  28
The Dead Don't Sin  30
What You Gave Me  32
What We Share  33
Poetry Workshop Exercise  34
An Exercise  35
Sunday Morning Jazz  36
Worship, Discovery and Reclamation  37
Listening  40
Still Howling  41
Endnote to Still Howling  50


Notes to the Poems  52

## Pure Poetry and Art

Once upon a time I thought
that the moments preceding death would be
a kaleidoscope of chakra colors framing images of my life:

fuchsia-violet, yellow, green and blue and indigo and red and
my daughter being born, her tiny
body emerging from mine,
she popping out like a cork from the finest champagne,
her birthing waters christening the room that
at once
filled with angels,
hundreds of angels
hovering about us,
and me seeing my baby's pure body and hearing her pure cry,
and me feeling love in the purest sense, the only sense
that love should be felt,
and me not knowing such pure poetry
again,
until my son . . .

red, indigo, green, yellow and blue and fuchsia-violet and
me hearing the sound of a weedeater
early one Saturday morning, thinking
it must be my neighbor, then
my seven-year-old son's small but firm grip
onto my sleep heavy hand.
*Mom, come and see what I made,* and me shuffling behind
his skip out the door to the front yard,
and the letters "M O M" carved large, heroic-sized,
perfectly across and into the front yard,
all the way down into the dirt,
inscribed into the earth,

and my son smiling so big, then me
dragging the ladder from the garage into the street
and climbing up it in my nightgown and robe
to get a panoramic view of my name weed eaten across the front yard,
and me standing near the top of that ladder, snapping
a photo of my son standing on the yard below,
one hand on his hip,
the other holding the weedeater I'd forbidden him to touch,
my son
standing proudly and firmly behind his art . . .

# Sun Shining Through

*Inspired by the painting* Sun Shining Through
*by Eric Wallis*

Sunday morning: the sun has risen to bless
all of Earth with its healing of light and heat.
She walks in her garden, stops to feel the sun
at her back, reveling in its pronouncement,
how it etches itself onto its flowers, its ferns,
its leaves, and her.

When she raises her arms behind her head
to the simple wooden barrette holding her hair
the sun shines through her thin white gown
making her position with the light look like wings
and celestial shine, a bodily halo, an aura: she appears
as an angel on Earth.
Only nature frames her.

Though she could, at any moment, raise her
arms higher and she would be gone, taken up
by the charm of the ethereal, her gaze keeps her
grounded. Underneath her sun-filled gown, she is
human.

She is thinking of him and of herself and of all
of Earth's children as she gazes to the life force
of our Mother. She sees the life that seemingly
magically and divinely-ordered springs from Her,
this parental planet that keeps us magnetically,
chemically, and genetically
bound to Her.

This angel's wings are not wings.
They are arms thinly covered
in the Earth's fabric made glistening and new
by this fresh day. She has chosen
to stay here, in this garden of life.
She lets down her hair.

## Prologue to Rosalind Franklin Speaks:

In awe, she sees
The gorgeous arrangement
From carefully photographing

The soon-to-be-famous
X-ray diffraction image.

She has discovered
The double helix.

Her findings are used
Without her permission.

Double Helix Triple Betrayal
By Watson, Crick and Wilkins.

## Rosalind Franklin Speaks

What is credited
and what is fact
are two strands
spiraling about one another,
to create all that we are,

holding the mysteries still to be revealed.

Discovery, that is what it is about.
Women are curious, too,
but, I am sorry, usually just not as damn selfish
for the recognition. We don't imprint our names
on our offspring or any of the next generation,
as we understand that engendered imprints are inherent,
not imposed, and uniqueness grows from heredity
rather than strong-armed control
and claims for what is not ours.
Forming the next generation in its
complex combination of what is
predicted, what is
unique,
is the DNA's job, not ours.

Certain that I wanted to
be a scientist at age 15,
I was able to get my
father, finally, to
allow me to study
what I am good at,
what defines me,
what courses in my blood,
what is in my DNA.

That took a lot of work,
just to get him to let
me be me, to study
my identity,
and yours.

And Father loved me.

What can I do about
Watson, Crick and Wilkins
who see women, even and
especially women of science,
through the eyes of their broken
x chromosome, the one we call
the y chromosome?

Take the discovery
that DNA is a double helix —
revealed by
my work,
my research,
my X-ray diffraction images,
my Photograph 51 —
and use it
without my knowledge
or permission.

Betrayal is nothing new.
Even my ovaries were in on it,
taking my life at age 37,
and four years later
giving the men the prize.

## Whose Art?

*Was the lady cast,*
Wrote Anita Pollitzer to Georgia O'Keeffe
On June 18, 1916
In reference to the sculpture Georgia had created
The month before, known as *Abstraction*, 1916.

Yes, the curved form of this sculpture
Viewed straight on
Resembles a figure, shrouded, head bowed —
A haunting femininity.

Some believe this could be an homage to her
Mother, who had just died.

I see a woman — I see a tribute.


Alfred Stieglitz supports her art —
He displays it in his New York gallery,
The same gallery that brought Matisse
To the U.S. even before the 1913 Armory Show.

With her help, he makes her famous.


He decides to use her in his art.
He depicts her in a photograph
Grasping her sculpture of a woman.

Viewed with his composition,
She appears as grasping a sculpture of a penis.

Woman usurped.

## Georgia O'Keeffe's *Black Iris III*, 1926

Contrasted like the yin yang,
*Black Iris III* is half dark
Half light.
Both are needed to make a whole,
To create completion.
This is a sacred coupling.

And what we see is sexual —
The graceful soft, soft folds —
A defining femininity.

To enter appears dark.
To leave appears dark.

But look how it illuminates from within.
       Within is where every human begins.
       This is a sacred illumination.

Within, a message awaits.

## Dream Animals

Which beast creeps in your dreams tonight, my love?
The bear again?  Yes, shaking its dusty hide

As it saunters from your pineal gland —
Brahma's cave or mother's womb,

Depending on whether tonight
You are a man or a boy.

Will its image paint your canvas
Or fashion its face into a mask?
What does your third eye see?

It's time to wake, before the
Owl swoops for you,
To take you deeper than dreams
And deeper
Than you wish to go.

## Clearstory

I

Even the moon wants
my peace

as it radiates full
through my clearstory windows.

Its splendor pries open my eyes, wanting me
to wake, to give it my attention.

The moon must be a man.

Men take the quiet.

They put their legs over me,
their arms tighten on my chest
like traps, and they press
their faces against my face, and

they snore in my ears.

They are big, heavy aggressors.

Before bed, they want my attention,
looking at me like sponges,
wanting me to smile, to
nod at every syllable,
wanting my intellectual property, and
to fill me with agendas, to
be and be and be what they want
me to be,
though they say I should always be me.

II

How can I be me when, with them, I am forgetting
how to sleep?

Once upon a time, hormones in their controlling lunacy
got me into this.

But happily ever after,
hormones packed their baggage and belongings
and their longings
and left,
but I am still here.

I have to get myself out.

I need sleep.

I need peace.

Why can't they just go
into the moonlight,
back to their caves,

and rock their genitals alone?

## A Wedding

But as my tiny body shook —
Under your awesome one of power —
Artfully parading in flight over me —
In freedom and pageantry I'd never before seen — I

Wanted you — I
Prayed even — That you would arch
And come to me —
To clutch me — Seize me — Possess me — Yes — Make me

Somehow completely yours —
For just one blazing second —

Then me —
Secure in your hold — Enchanted
By the danger — of you poised over my fur and skin — I
Felt the glint from your black eye —

As you cocked your head —
And it was in that one — blazing — second — I
Understood what marriage to you meant — You
Plunged your greedy beak into my heart — I

Died —
And married you anyway.

## 2 a.m. Snowflakes in March in New Mexico

For some reason, we are closing down
The bar. We are not drinking, so what got us here
Must have been the band and the fact
That we wanted to get out of the room
Where I was, once again, breaking up with you.

It is 2 a.m. and late March in New Mexico.
We are out on the street heading for the car,
And the sky opens and pieces of heaven
Begin falling on us, blessing us with
Their loveliness and purity.

We laugh at the wonder of how huge
These snowflakes are.
Even though I am from the Midwest I have
Never seen such large snowflakes as these.
You are from here, and neither have you.

Maybe they only fall this way at the end
Of the night near the beginning of the day,
And we, in bed cuddling each other
At that hour, have missed this Eighth Wonder.

Driving to my place, we continue
To marvel at their intricately-carved incredibly
Great beauty covering our slow pace.

We arrive
And park, and outside my door
We laugh some more, and, yes, admire
Their individuality that is so pronounced
We can see it with the naked eye.

Neighbors who are still awake, either
Alone or as couples after making love or fighting
Or just being

Together as couples,
Join us on the sidewalk;
We all look up in admiration and joy.

You and I open our mouths and catch
What we can. We savor these pieces
Of Heaven-baked manna.

Our hair and lashes and faces glisten
With the landing of our snowflakes. We
Go inside. Back in the room that earlier
We had so desperately wanted to leave, we
Lie together, holding each other
And watch through the sliding glass doors
The snowflakes that continue
To grace the late night early morning sky.


Remembering that night and us, I want
To tell you this:

I wanted to love you, and not less
Than the way you loved me, accepting me
Completely for who I am.
I love you, but not in that way.

As large as those snowflakes were,
Still there were spaces between them,
Spaces of essence.

This is what I know —
        I love you like the spaces between
        And through each flake of snow,

        The spaces that define each falling gift
        And make each as individual
        As an individual.

You added the dance of moisture
To the parched New Mexico sky.

# Canvas of Life, Look Closely

*Inspired by the painting Hope*
*by Steve Dezember II,*
*depicted on the cover of this book.*

"At first, when I learned I had ALS,
I was resentful, and then,
I realized,
I didn't want to live my life that way."
   Steve Dezember II

"You take what life gives you
And you make it work."
   Hope Cross Dezember

I

From a distance
The painting is beautiful, abstract, non-representational.

It is a swirl of colors — like life —
And bursting through the midst of it all
What could be
A white flower — white rose on rose.
To me, this symbolizes hope,
A quality that doesn't come automatically with life;

We must find hope.

Move closer — look closely,
See the swirls? What do they look like?

Yes, wheel tracks.
They are the prints of my nephew Steve.

What else do you see?

Walking with the wheel prints
Are the prints of Hope.


II


Hope steps in stride with us if we allow
And don't insist on painting
Alone.


III


In August 2011, when Steve was 28, ALS found him.
Steve and Hope married two months later.

By 2013, Steve had lost almost all motor skills,
Including the ability to speak with a voice,
But he could move his lips.
Hope read his lips and spoke his words.

In 2015, after acquiring a communication device
And through social media, Steve planned a surprise
Birthday party for his wife.

In August 2016, Steve exceeded the limits
And defied the doctor dictates of five years to live.

IV


In spite of it all,
He creates.
And he loves.

As stated on driveforacure.com and hopeforsteve.com:

"ALS has taken a lot from Steve including his ability to move,
eat or even breathe on his own, but it has not taken his
drive for life or his ability to drive his wheelchair."

Steve's paintings, the websites state, are "an expression
of the creative freedom Steve still experiences, his drive
to keep fighting and to share his love."


V


Steve + Hope.

They could complain.
They could resent.
They don't.

Instead, they use what they have
To create
Beauty
And meaning
And inspiration.

They are artists
Of the canvas of life.

## Walking a Bridge of Fire

*For my mom*
*For my nephew*
*For my brothers and my dad*

*In honor of all of the valiant*
*And their lives*
*And as a reminder to me*


Walking a bridge of fire
Dancing barefoot on Denali peak
Resisting tornadoes with a fist
Scaling Everest on crutches
Skating ice caps in a wheelchair


    — teeth knocked out ribs and kneecaps snapped in half
    eyes slashed
    by speeding metal and splintering glass
    from the impact of that oncoming car, turning
    to look through the blur at your loves stunned
    and scared in the back seat
    and smiling now toothless at them, your children,
    asking
    *how are you, children?*
    trying to comfort and soothe
    your little boy, your little girl
    through your face of blood —


Saying *no* to disease, *no* to injury, *no* to pain
While asking each — because each has wings —
*why were you sent? and what can you tell me?*
And, after listening,
Saying *thank you, now go*

Saying yes to poetry
Saying yes to our breasts
Saying yes to our brains
Saying yes to our legs, feet, ankles and arms
Saying yes to our tracheas, lungs and nerves
Saying yes to our pancreases, livers, kidneys and prostates
Saying yes to our ovaries, uteruses, vaginas and fallopian tubes
Saying yes to our bodies
Saying yes to our lives
Saying yes to vibrancy and to stamina
Saying yes to our hearts

Saying yes as each sun rises,
Feeling that celestial life-protecting body
Draw light from the dark
To alert all earth

Saying yes petal by petal

Saying yes to conviction and faith
Saying yes to this moment
Defying limits and statistics and
Saying no to certain things while
Saying yes
Saying yes
Saying yes  yes  yes
To everything else

## The Dead Don't Sin

What I call it now is survival.
I used to call it greed, evil, lust.
I used to call it sin.
That's because I was dead,
And the dead don't sin.
The dead do nothing.
Nothing.
The really dead don't even rot.
That was me.
I was hooked and hung in a freezer.
Then he walked in.

He was different than the others.
He didn't have a cleaver
In those hands of his – those hands
That blessed first the parts that most just take,
The parts he gave back to me
By the warmth of his palms pressed to them.

My dull eyes opened
And nearly blistered in the cold.
He lifted me off and held me
Until I was warm enough on my own.

It was then I began to sin.
I ran from the freezer
And danced my nakedness before him.
I asked him to devour me.
I begged to devour him.
(After being dead so long,
I was hungry.
Hungry.)

He said, "No. There are other ways to fill
Our souls."
Then he took off his silver raincoat
And draped it around me.

## What You Gave Me

You were so cool,
wearing your Surfers Cross,
tanned and so cute,
J. C.,
my 4th grade boyfriend:

Part of everything
the desert around my home
in Paradise Valley gave —
arched sunlight
carving rocks into mountains,
long expanses of land and sky
for running and flying,
beautiful days every day,
coyotes howling me to sleep.

I would hold onto what you gave me
when at the next
stop
of a single-blooded country town in Indiana
no one understood me
or my tan that soon melted
or my pimples that covered my face
like a farmland.

What you gave me,
I still have:
the numbers 007
carved in an eraser.

## What We Share

Lying on your back and gazing to the sky, focus
On the breaks between tree leaves,
The crystalline kaleidoscope of ever-present sunlight,
Stashing its stash of purity and color.
Light appears to claim no color,
But is violet, indigo, blue, green, yellow, orange, red,
And all the human hues and human merging,
Renditions of those colors.
Light is all colors.

And then there is pink.
Pink is the color of not flesh, but tongues.
Pink sings its music from the tongues of all people,
Blending its love and life and breath
Into the sunrise.

# Poetry Workshop Exercise

1. Write three nouns as fast as you can.

2. Write three nouns about nature.

3. Describe a mirror with three adjectives.

4. Describe an ocean with three adjectives.

5. In one sentence, describe your perfect day.

6. Use the above sentence as either the first or last line of your poem.

7. Use all nouns and adjectives in your poem.

## An Exercise

Reflective, I push away my coffee cup,
Rise from my chair
And leave my desk:

I am drawn to the outdoors.

I join the trees, sky, grass:
They are so kind, non-judgmental, peaceful.

Lying in the grass
And gazing past the tree into the sky,
I observe:

Life is vast and mysterious.

I realize it is necessary that I push past
The boundary to my potential:

Yes, I slept until I woke.

Now I hike, write,
Laugh with my children,
And breathe.

# Sunday Morning Jazz

Swaying her hips, twisting her torso,
A woman moves toward
The band, then back —

Long strands swirl about her neck.

Through the window
Water shines clear,
Shaking, shimmering
On the lattice of iron.

Fluid though bound,
Black is cupped by white.

And all I want
Is to be seen with fresh eyes.

## Worship, Discovery and Reclamation

I

When he worships with her, the way he parts her hair
and the places beneath
in adoration,
she likes to watch him,
the questions on his face as he begins
his pilgrimage with his fingers,
looking for satisfaction — answers,
   maybe as to his        very own beginning.

          Man.
          His beginning.
        How he likes to begin
          again and again.

She wonders, where do I begin — and where do you end? And what am I, as I watch you kneel before me, your eyes seeking their origin? She tells herself that maybe she will capture the words this time, as her eyes close and she lets him define her in the way that he does, with his tongue outlining her then filling her. Finally, when she joins him, she
        ohdearGod
        finds again
        finds again
        finds again
      that their sounds,
    theirs, yet somehow distant,
   are cryptic enough to carve the
olympic rocks of an earth-bound Sedona canyon

    but they do not tell the story.

After, when his fingers comb her hair
and calm the places beneath
like breezes through wheat
that make a gentle ocean without the water,
without the moon,
she wants to sing, very soft, a folk song –
the story that waits beyond this –
though she is not the one who has the melody or the words.


II

When he says God oh God, she knows that he is praying.  She can't help thinking how it wasn't always this way.  She recalls the years of nights when he'd come to bed with her, she knew for sex, just sex, and she hated it really, hated him really, but she couldn't tell him, because she had never told herself.  Then after, he'd say if she didn't mind, he had the newspaper to finish, so alone she fell asleep.  No, she was already asleep.  No, she was dead.

And then she remembers how the old twin mattress stuffed in the trunk of his car stuck out too far, and how she, in her car, followed him just in case the mattress fell out, and how he carried it up the steps to his hollow apartment, and how she undressed in front of him because, oddly, she wanted sex, and just that. And after, she dressed in front of him and left him, driving to the house and the life she made him leave and she claimed. When she got home, she didn't read the paper. She wrote a poem.

That was then. Now, watching him rest beside her, she writes a new poem, and she calls it "Our Poem."

# III

## Our Poem

As you rest now next to me, your fingertips retracing me then
filling me in, you tell me how you understand why we have
each other, how not only do we get to feel each other
and the glory of that, but how also God gives as
my flesh gives when your fingers journey me.
You look at my face and you ask me what
I am thinking about. I say I don't want
to be your goddess or your
angel or your wife. I don't
want to be your mother.
I say I could be your
friend. I could be
your lover. You
say what you
want me to
be is me.
I say I
am a
poet.

## Listening

Birds — two different species
Filling space more frequently

Repetitious bird words

Another sound approaches

Louder
Louder

Some type of machinery
Sharing the bird song's space

Ah!  A train whistle.

Now, coyotes whine
And whine and whine

Yet — the train!  Its whistle says,

"I'm King!"

But a single bird persists . . .

*Poet's Note: This poem and "Endnote to Still Howling" are an homage to
Allen Ginsberg and to his poems "Howl" and "Footnote to Howl"
and a tribute to his publisher, City Lights Publishers,
and to Allen's influences, namely Walt Whitman,
but mostly to Allen and what he gave us —*

*the right to howl.*

## Still Howling

*For Galaxy Dancer*

I

I see the best souls of my sex thrive despite the madness,
      defiant Aphrodites rising above the sea,
naked in their wakefulness, determined to love in the charge of night
      and the terror of the day,
deciding once again to abandon the search for the soulful man
      after yet another set of promisepromisepromise
      tips the dominos of stated love
      into a dynamic display of arcane art,
      cascading into a fluid falling
      of each word promisepromisepromise caress kiss
      fuck
      from the men
who, for three weeks, call and text and relentlessly
      text and change
      their plans so they can drive across town
      and fly across continents to see us
      only to soon mysteriously forever disappear,

who devote their lives to a higher calling, meditate, pray then
        lash out angrily when we ask a question,
who, while holding our hands and kissing our cheeks verbally twist
        our arms behind our backs and nip our cheeks,
        holding mirrors to our faces and ranting at us
        that we are their relentless demanding debilitated mothers,
who have environmentally-safe companies, off-grid homes,
        and work against proliferation to keep the world a place,
        sitting late into the night with grieving families,
but slam the gavel to the bench in the pronouncement
        that we are selfish and demanding when we ask to be held
        after a day we spent helplessly watching human sacrifices by
        the gods of business and have realized finally that each
        sacrifice was us,
who vow they will be there for us but won't return calls or texts
        even when our closest family member has just died,
who have children they want us to raise, children whose mothers
        escaped through the vacuum cleaner,
who, with blood perpetually drying under their fingernails,
        doggedly beget war,
        marching our courageous and caring
        sons and daughters
        into the family business and even into its copiers and
        shredders,
who bring prison with them in their assertion they were protecting
        their families from invaders, dealers, and the IRS,
who visit the Dali Lama, chant on mountain tops,
        embrace the dawn of the equinox on the apex of a Sedona
        rock in the midst of a vortex
        by running up their wives' credit cards then vanish
        into the evening mist,
who profess their love but refuse to hide their dating profiles on
        matchdotcom, okcupid, greensingles, matchmaker,
        loveforever dot org, dot net, dot com, dot com,
        dot we do not communicate,
claiming these are mere social networking sites,

        they just want to meet new friends,
            and say we are selfish and have no right to expect their
            profiles to be hidden, and, by asking, have now ruined the
            perfect night of sex and spooning we just shared,
who meet us for coffee and after only this once, because we don't
        want to meet them again, call and text and email inexorably,
        harassing us with venom and nasty,
who hit us in the adolescent classroom, calling us crater face
        because we mature with pimples,
who bully with questions and accusations every time we step outside
        our doors,
who tell us what to do with our homes, yards, jobs, lives, children and
        claim they are just being neighborly,
who boldly ask us to come to Boulder, and we drive to Boulder, and
        after we arrive in Boulder, they no longer want to see us,
        and we sleep alone in a sad motel in Boulder,
who with sweet breath of desire tell us they will count the times we
        make love, then
        we discover they can only count to one,
who patiently date us laugh touch kiss and smile for a few months, no
        sex yet, so we can be sure, then after finally making love say
        this was a mistake,
who on our honeymoons say this was a mistake, no not the trip
        to the tropics or the tower or the falls, we are the mistake,
who, with fatherly, brotherly, uncle-y advice, tell us we are naive and
        stupid to believe what men say,
and we wonder what kind of world this is
        that gives the message to males that it is smart to lie
        but gives the message to females that we are stupid to
        believe men, *stupid, stupid, stupid, I believed him* –
        how about the message to everyone that your word
        should be true and on your honor so you can be honorable?
who see us as prey when we reach age 10, taking our childhood,
        never do we get to be a non-sexualized person,
who, on occasion, stop leaking faucets, kill people-devouring spiders
        but freely distribute advice, solutions, STDs ... and babies –

ah, Galaxy, we are not safe, but we are resilient, in ways that our
    mothers from forever
    past must have also known,
as they forgave while being burned at the stake, their flesh
    searing,
    prayed before putting their heads to the block, bracing
    before being slammed and ripped with the furious steel rod
    weapon,
    which made the ripping and hand-muffled
    screaming beyond the limits of what should be known,
    escaping into a mental abyss before thuds and blows to the
    faces,
    blows to the stomachs, blows to the breasts,
    blowblowblow
and too much of that still happens to our sisters.


II

And what of our daughters?

The Machinery of Balls, soccer balls, baseballs, volleyballs,
    golf balls, tennis balls, rugby balls, racket balls,
    balls balls balls and of hockey pucks, of fucks
    and of cock
    built of titanium and diamond, built in the basement labs
    of Los Alamos and sometimes in homes,
    is nearly invisible — it takes eyes beyond the spiritual to see
    it; it is easier to feel it,
and now that our daughters are allowed to run on courts and fields,
    they sense this Machinery with a mixture of caution and
    familiarity
    and even guardianship,
    and we, the mothers, sisters and aunts,

want to warn, inform and protect them and to protect men, too,
        because men, too, are caught in this Machinery,
and we have sons and grandsons and brothers and fathers and
        grandfathers and nephews and cousins and uncles and
        friends whom we love,
and it occurs to me that we are all of this Machinery, I am of it, too;
        it is the world of balls, for the world is a ball, too, in a
        universe of balls,
        some are hot, searing, rotating, some appear cold and static,
        but a Machinery of Balls like
        the pitching machine, and we must
        be prepared, as our daughters are prepared, to swing to
        survive the blows when the
Pitching Machine starts pitching softballs slowly, in the fragrance
        of the morning air, dew still freshening the space around the
        cage, we still slender in our short white shorts,
        we are ready to learn the game,
Pitching Machine quickens as balls spin toward us, we batting at
        them, deflecting some and dodging most, and the Machine's
        arm shoots, then shoots, then shoots
        more rapidly, balls shoot at us ballsballsballs
        ballsballsballs and what has happened to this fucking machine
        it is broken and relentless in throwing balls at us
        and these are hard balls, balls of iron, of steel, of stone, of
        titanium and muscle, rarely of diamond,
thud thud thud thud thud to the head and we are locked in the cage
        and bruised by balls but we are still standing
thud to the breast, thud thud thud to the heart, thud again to the
        heart,
thud to the thighs, thud to the pubics, and now red
        stains our white shorts and we start to howl,
        and I am still howling as the
Pitching Machine pitches more hardballs, then it starts pitching
        soccer balls, tennis balls, racquet balls, golf balls,
        and everything spherical —

        marbles, oranges, furiously at us comes balls of yarn,
        snow balls, and a planet called Cockland, pitched at us,
        and we take it, the world we know,
        the whole planet of Cockland,
        absorbing Cockland into our blood,
and my daughter says there are too many balls in my poem,
        and she's right, that is exactly the point,
        there are too many balls in my poem.


## III

Galaxy Dancer! I'm with you in Cockland
        where you've stayed saner than I have
I'm with you in Cockland
        where we love men yes we do
        and we love their bodies geometric hard muscular
        the safety of chests and the thrill of erections
I'm with you in Cockland
        where I spend one more night in bed
        with my computer and my cat and with Allen and with Walt
        and his loving bedfellow God
I'm with you in Cockland
        where I thank Allen and Allen knows
        that I am grateful that he gave us this form to express
        ourselves and my bra's off to you Allen and this is an
        homage for I am alive serious and I know you will cheer
        for me from Heaven where this poem is published with
        yours and many others because you gave us the form
        that I at this moment christen
        The Howl Form
        and you gave us the right the freedom to howl so that we
        too can howl

And don't you reader or listener in the audience
>	have at least one thing to Howl about?  So let's sing our
>	praises of thanksgiving
>	to Allen by howling which I am doing by Still Howling

I'm with you in Cockland
>	where I thank Walt and Walt knows
>	don't you Walt that I am thankful for the free long-legged
>	long-winded long-armed lines circling and hugging our
>	waists and embracing the expansive freedom to express
>	freely and expansively in repetitious verse

I'm with you in Cockland
>	where the system and its people and our
>	fathers husbands brothers uncles co-workers supervisors
>	bosses lovers and friends still have 525,600 ways
>	to tell us to shut up which is one way for each minute of
>	each day of each new year

I'm with you in Cockland
>	where men and women have given and continue to give
>	their lives in courtrooms and prisons and to death so that
>	we can be free
>	to write and speak and howl even if
>	the words are about Cockland

I'm with you in Cockland
>	where we love men love men love men
>	love them love men we do
>	but just because we love them so much doesn't mean
>	we need to be quiet

I'm with you in Cockland
>	where once a famous male poet
>	after hearing me read poems now in my debut book of
>	poetry said *You are writing a new kind of female poetry:*
>	*It is obvious you've been hurt by men, but you love them.*
>	*You are not writing angry poetry*
>	and it is true: I am not angry
>	I am just saying

I'm with you in Cockland
> where I am just saying where you are just saying
> where he is just saying where she is just saying where we all
> can just say  though I once was quiet and still as a little
> mouse while inside I was howling  but because of
> Allen and the City Lights that are the brightest I am now
> howling and I am no longer still for I am loud howling and
> with this I am Still Howling

I'm with you in Cockland
> because for now this is the only place
> to live our lives and life is amazing incredible beautiful
> regenerative exciting shining and glorious
> and even in Cockland this is my moment
> this is your moment and no one can take the glory of that
> unless we give it to them

I'm with you in Cockland
> where I will die and I am not afraid to die
> I just prefer to live

I'm with you in Cockland
> my sister
> where you persevere
> come what may
> without real health care with few opportunities
> with no more than minimum wage yes still working harder
> than our male counterparts for less
> recognition and less pay
> we survive on crumbs falling from the master's table but we
> are not lap dogs and we are making our way
> to speak at the banquet and to remake
> the table so that it is round

I'm with you in Cockland
> where we hug and kiss and caress our men
> in the beds they've made
> the men who snore all night and won't let us sleep

Men, keep your underpants on, we're free! We've had enough of
    Cockland. Try giving us something new and find within you a
    nakedness and love that manifests in ways beyond the body,
    way beyond the cock.

My soul-full infinite sister,

I'm with you in Cockland,
    where I see you dancing above me through the galaxies,
    weaving barefoot tracks in the cosmos
    and in the celestial sand
    as you continue your universal global coastal dance
    to my skiff, moored on the shore
    of the un-navigable ocean of *hegemonous* men.

*Albuquerque, 2011 – 2016*

## Endnote to Still Howling

Forgive, forgive, forgive, forgive, forgive, forgive, forgive, forgive,
        forgive, forgive, forgive, forgive.
The body needs forgiveness, the mind needs forgiveness, even
        the good ole soul in all its devoted goodness, lamenting
        and loneliness needs forgiveness, and the spirit,
        crazy journeyer, needs
        forgiveness.
Forgiveness is a different Realm.
        We are here to populate that Realm.
Forgiveness helps everyone, the world, each cell of our being
        human,
For what are we without forgiveness?
        Yes, what are we without forgiveness?
Beasts that tear at one another, digging for the heart with our
        incisors, digging to destroy the heart of the other, digging
        and tearing
        into our own hearts?
And in spite of being trained to believe otherwise,
        humans do not have to be beasts —
        we are not animals; we are human, meaning humane.
        Break training: Forgive.
We hurt one another; in spite of our best attempts to do otherwise,
        it happens — we hurt one another, so
Forgive and create a space for connection and for breathing
        and for not walking on a planet of broken shells;
        instead,
        let's walk on oceans.
Humans, let humans be human.
        Man, Woman, the human step is compassion.
        The superhuman step is forgiveness,
        And then, Superman, Superwoman, we fly.
        We're closer to the divine than we know.

Forgive and forgive.

Forgive everyone, and everything, that makes you want to
    howl.
Forgive everyone, and everything, that makes you howl.
    Forgive Cockland in all of its self-made glory.
    Cockland, forgive.

Forgiveness is the vehicle to the Land of Miracles —
    Forgive and be
    the alchemy.

Ask to be forgiven.
    Yes, ask others to forgive you.

Forgive life and what life gives you.

Forgive God.

Forgiveness releases you
    and gives you song.

Practice forgiveness with every breath
    so that at the moment preceding death
    you will be forgiving.

Mostly,
    look into the mirror and say,
    I forgive you; I love you,

Then live in the miracle
    of love's reflection.

*Albuquerque, 2014 - 2016*

# Notes to the Poems

### "Pure Poetry and Art"
My daughter Elaine still attracts hundreds of angels that fill whatever space she is in. She is a writer, a visual artist, an arts educator, an innovator and an entrepreneur. You can read about her business at sightprojects.com and santafearttours.com.

My son Sean continues to stand proudly and firmly behind his art by being a writer, a rapper, a musician, an innovator and an entrepreneur of a motivational speaking and rapping business. You can read about his business at seanritchel.com.

All five of my children excel in their passions and continue, as always and in all ways, to bless my life with joy and love.

### "Sun Shining Through"
"Sun Shining Through" is inspired by the painting by Eric Wallis entitled *Sun Shining Through;* this painting is depicted on the cover of my debut book of poetry, *Earth-Marked Like You,* published by Sunstone Press.

### "Prologue to Rosalind Franklin Speaks:" and "Rosalind Franklin Speaks"
Information about Dr. Rosalind Franklin is from "Rosalind Elsie Franklin: Pioneer Molecular Biologist," *Women in Science: A Selection of 16 Significant Contributors,* The San Diego Supercomputer Center, and from Biography.com Editors, "Rosalind Franklin Biography," The Biography.com website, published by A & E Television Networks.

### "Whose Art?"
Information about Georgia O'Keeffe and Anita Pollitzer is from *Georgia O'Keeffe* by Lisa Mintz Messinger, Thames & Hudson world of art, 2001, and from *Lovingly, Georgia: The Complete Correspondence of Georgia O'Keeffe & Anita Pollitzer*, Edited by Clive Giboire, Introduction by Benita Eisler, A Touchstone Book, Simon & Schuster, 1990. Drawings of women with similar curved forms to *Abstraction,* 1916, grace a letter from Georgia to Anita dated December 1915, as shown in *Lovingly Georgia: The Complete Correspondence of Georgia O'Keeffe & Anita Pollitzer.*

### "Dream Animals"
Relationship of the bear, Brahma's cave, womb and pineal gland is from *Medicine Cards: The Discovery of Power Through the Ways of Animals* by Jamie Sams & David Carson, Illustrated by Angela C. Werneke, Bear & Company, 1988.

### "Canvas of Life, Look Closely"
Please read more about this inspiring and creative couple, Steve and Hope, at hopeforsteve.com and driveforacure.com.

### "Still Howling"
This poem could not have been possible without the influence of the poem "Howl" by Allen Ginsberg, published by City Lights Publishers in *Howl and Other Poems*. Please read Allen's powerful poem.

Galaxy Dancer, Ph.D., is a guide in life passages, theater arts, and writing. You can read more about her and the vision quest and rites of passage programs she leads at owlandhawkpassages.com.

### "Endnote to Still Howling"
This poem could not have been possible without the influence of the poem "Footnote to Howl" by Allen Ginsberg, published by City Lights Publishers in *Howl and Other Poems*. Please read his powerful poem.

Made in United States
Orlando, FL
02 April 2024